LaunchPad for *Introducing Psychology*, Fifth Edition

Available December 2020 at launchpadworks.com

Each chapter in LaunchPad for *Introducing Psychology*, Fifth Edition, features a collection of activities carefully chosen to help master the major concepts. The site serves students as a comprehensive online study guide, available any time, with opportunities for self-quizzing with instant feedback, exam preparation, and further explorations of topics from the textbook. For instructors, all units and activities can be instantly assigned and students' results and analytics are collected in the Gradebook.

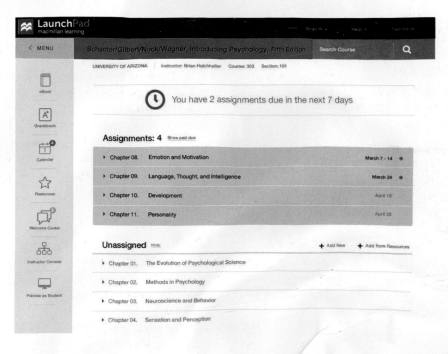

For Students

- Full e-book of *Introducing Psychology*, Fifth Edition
- LearningCurve Quizzing
- Student Video Activities
- Data Visualization Activities
- Concept Practice Activities
- PsychSim 6.0 by Thomas Ludwig and John Krantz

For Instructors

- Gradebook
- Presentation Slides
- iClicker Questions
- Chapter Figures and Photos
- Correlation of *Introducing Psychology*, Fifth Edition, to APA Learning Goals
- Correlation of *Introducing Psychology*, Fifth Edition, to MCAT Topics